The Cosmic Purr

The Cosmic Purr

POEMS BY

Aaron Poochigian

ABLE MUSE PRESS

Able Muse Press

www.ablemusepress.com

Printed in the United States of America

Library of Congress Control Number: 2011944930

ISBN 978-0-9878705-2-0

Foreword copyright ©2012 by Charles Martin

Cover image: *Eclipse Time Lapse* by Jacqueline Barkla

Cover & book design by Alexander Pepple

Able Muse Press is an imprint of *Able Muse:* A Review of Poetry, Prose & Art—at
www.ablemuse.com

Able Muse Press
467 Saratoga Avenue #602
San Jose, CA 95129

Acknowledgments

The author gratefully acknowledges the publications in which these poems (sometimes under different titles or in slightly different versions) first appeared:

Able Muse: "Grand Forks, ND," "The Long Window."
American Arts Quarterly: "Captain Meriwether Lewis and the Great Falls."
Arion: "Helen's *Iliad,*" "The Marriage of Peleus and Thetis."
Barefoot Muse: "In His Beak an Olive Branch."
Chronogram: "Well, Since You Asked. . . ."
Classical Outlook: "Antiphon," "The Mystes."
Poetry: "The Vigil."
Raintown Review: "The Stage Designer," "Torque."
Smartish Pace: "To My Soul Mate," "The Last Bachelors."
The Dark Horse: "Medusa," "Reunion Show," "Pulling the Wagon," "Utah Adieu," "To the Bride, in the Dressing Room."
The Financial Times: "Some call ships, infantry or horsemen."
The Flea: "The Mentor."
The Waywiser Anthology: "Kudzu."
Think Journal: "Chumps."
Unsplendid: "Matter."

Foreword

The appearance of Aaron Poochigian's *The Cosmic Purr* marks the debut of a poet of distinctive voice and impressive formal accomplishment. It is unusual these days for a young poet in an M.F.A. program to emerge from it with the kind of skill that Poochigian displays here; often enough poets seem to be able to get through such programs without learning much at all about the uses of metrical verse. It should be no surprise then to learn that Poochigian has avoided the M.F.A. route in favor of getting a Ph.D. in Classics, and while this is his first book of his own poetry, he has honed his metrical chops on the production of excellent translations of the plays of Aeschylus, the *Phaenomena* of Aratus, and the lyric poems and fragments of Sappho.

As a young man in Minnesota, he studied the craft of poetry with three poets notable for their employment of traditional means: David Mason, Timothy Murphy, and Alan Sullivan. In the first section of *The Cosmic Purr* Poochigian pays tribute to Sullivan in a poem called "The Mentor":

You were a man intolerant of nonsense.
Your voice dug in, expanded, and became my conscience.
Now you shock me from beyond the grave.
I should be grateful someone's still around to save
my moron forays from the Mire of Lies.
Truth is, every time a real hard-ass dies
the brunt of him doesn't just go away.
Truth is, you live on, killing all I shouldn't say.

Many poets of Poochigian's generation would no doubt find these sentiments the rankest heresy, but the discipline of a younger poet's ear comes from absorbing the lessons of an older poet's voice, and to speak of that knowledge as forming a conscience seems no more than accurate. This may not be the only conscience that the younger poet needs, but without it there is little chance of his being able to form a consistent voice of his own. Just as a conscience cannot tell us what to do, but only what not to do, the conscience formed by the mentor's voice can only tell the poet what he should not say. The killing Poochigian speaks of is a form of liberation for the younger poet: where the mentor leaves off, there the poet begins.

What follows is an act of poetic self-creation, attended, in an age like ours when everything is possible and little seems to matter, by a considerable degree of anxiety. Few poets would have the skill to allegorize that anxiety in a poem as subtly hilarious as Poochigian's "Places, Places":

Two minutes, people . . . wait, hold, hold for ten.
Boots clomp and flounces rustle in distress:
the leading man has passed out drunk again.
And who are you? You'll have to do, I guess.

No use resisting—practiced hands have stripped me
and crammed my toes, hams, haunches into hose.
What lines, what cues, what songs? They have equipped me
only with rapier and mustachios.

Showtime. A hush blows in and lights discover
the cardboard forest where I must fool all
the people, all, at least till curtain call.

And then one step as hero, fop or lover,
and I have stumbled from the dream. It's dawn.
The setting is my own. The show goes on.

It isn't easy to become the one that one imagines: circumstances
conspire to delay the process, as in the no less theatrical "Our Town,"
where the flatness of quotidian reality retards the drama:

Where was the *jeune premier?* The aproned ingénue?
Would they appear and air
big dreams, grand schemes, the regional despair?
No, not this evening. They had chores to do.

Reluctance like a curtain coming down
smothered the lark, and there it was, our town
again, a blip vanishing into prairie. . . .

A theme frequently tapped into in this book is that of the tension
between being one and being one with another, the latter theme

also explored in a theatrical setting of "The Stage Designer," where "the too enticing wife in silk brocade" is first fallen for and then fled from:

> She spoke so well I had my own designs
> until a sudden husband came to get her,
> and that was it. *Good night.* (I cut some lines.)
>
> And off they drove back to their own routines
> and I to mine, and life may well be better
> without the drama, the big ugly scenes.

In a sense, quality of life is the issue here, and whether we are better off without the big scenes, the grand passions, or merely impoverished, is a question that Poochigian keeps coming around to. He is nothing if not ambivalent about the issue, and moves from one side ("These so-called weddings, how can they be real?") to the other, often in the same poem: "Today the single cynic feels persuasion / urging one plus one is one." These last lines come from "One Plus One: A Wedding Sermon." Several of Poochigian's poems are set at weddings, another form of public ritual not unlike the theater. These provide him with another arena in which to dramatize the tension between the One and the Other, self-sufficiency and commitment. My favorite of these is "To the Bride, in the Dressing Room," a tour de force in impeccably rhymed dimeter quatrains, wherein Poochigian, impersonating a disappointed suitor, explores the symbology of traditional marriages while simultaneously dealing with a last-minute change of heart by the bride, who appears to be making an offer that, for one reason or another, he can only refuse. The poem ends with the speaker backing away from her invitation:

No, it's too late.
No, it's nothing.

You will find me outside,
eyes wet with the grit
that kept the bride
immaculate.

Somewhere off in the shadows, the spirits of James Merrill and Ovid bow in unison and silently applaud.

Not to mention Sappho. It's become fashionable lately to argue that translation of the classics cannot have the same importance to our poetry that it had in the period from, say, Christopher Marlowe to Alexander Pope, when translators in part created English poetry by the act of Englishing Ovid or Homer. That is true enough, but there are other lessons to be learned from translating the classics that can still enrich our poetry. From his translation of Sappho (and surely from his reading of Catullus as well) Poochigian has learned how to imagine the audience of his poem not only within it (as the bride is in "To the Bride In the Dressing Room") but actually interacting with the speaker. The reader will notice how many of the poems use the first person plural and address a nameless "you" who dutifully disappears, allowing the reader entry into the poem. In a time when many poets do not appear to be talking to anyone at all, Poochigian's direct address is more than refreshing.

Aaron Poochigian is both a classicist and a neo-classical poet. By this I mean that he prefers as subjects the common occasions of our lives and articulates them uncommonly, in verse rich with the kind of detail that becomes a style passed on in an act of friendship between him and the poets of the past who have served as his mentors. That is one meaning of the word 'traditional.' The limits of that style are not seen as contradicting in any way the creative energies of the poet. Rather, the poet gains force by allegorizing those limits and the struggle against them. In the last poem of *The Cosmic Purr,* Poochigian creates a scene ("A dusty dancing floor, a paneled screen / painted like a façade . . .") in which Death approaches the Matron waiting to give her last performance, "because she must be dying soon / and needs to speak her piece before she goes." Poochigian knows that she will die, even as we all will, but he also knows that in the intricate knot of utterance made by the poem, mortality can be held at bay. Here is the second, concluding stanza of "Death and the Matron":

> God bless the lady—she will go down talking
>   as if each passage were her last,
> a swan singing a filibuster, blocking
>   the *coup de grâce.* One moment in suspense
> spiraling outward into eloquence,
>   the plot curls up and dozes; Death stops stalking
>   and stands with the supporting cast.
>   It's too late now, she's bound us fast
> with long sentences, coiled magnificence.

—Charles Martin

CONTENTS

The Light at Troy

I declare
that later on,
even in an age unlike our own,
someone will remember who we are.

Sappho

Americana

Grand Forks, ND

To make it back home for the holidays,
Interstate Twenty-nine, a black ice glaze:
the smokestacks at the Crystal Sugar Plant
spouting the only mountains, tumbledown
slaughterhouses, barns sagging aslant,
and homesteads under heaps like winter wheat—
scant signs of life, and, goddamn, several feet
of fresh obscurity have blurred the town.

What now? The Mustang hung up in a ditch,
there's no choice but an outside world in which
hinged things are creaking—car doors, elbows, knees.
But all is calm now that the wind has fallen.
Time slows down as in epiphanies.
Breath swirls and swirls away. I had forgotten
snowflakes could float about like this, like cotton
from cottonwoods, like tufts of crystal pollen.

Our Town

Like houselights dimming in a theater
the sunset was a signal: drama would occur.
Street lamps here and there
spotlit familiar objects in the square—
some benches, a swing set—as if they were
of consequence. The sprinklers hushed on cue.
Where was the *jeune premier?* The aproned ingénue?
Would they appear and air
big dreams, grand schemes, the regional despair?
No, not this evening. They had chores to do.

Reluctance like a curtain coming down
smothered the lark, and there it was, our town
again, a blip vanishing into prairie,
and no roads leading to the luminary
metropolis where life was all night long
drinking and dancing, bursting into song.

After Bar

When their friends had dissolved in that festival air,
they were each, it emerged, what the other had got.
Like a nod and a shrug, like the wings of a dare,
there was harmony. Logic was *why the hell not?*

So they strolled, and Manhattan itself had a hand in
escorting them, holding mechanical doors.
The express train jostled about with abandon;
the lift in an instant surmounted the floors.

If the pad was a horror of crumbling plaster,
the dimmer respectfully whisked it from sight,
and the windows were pictures some pointillist master
had stippled with infinite twinges of light.

It was city they reached for—a hustler, a sequined
seductress, a compound of money and musk,
an extravagant mood, a perpetual weekend,
a fantasy turned on at dusk.

Reunion Show

Remember rage the way we used to love it
and what mad masks we wore when we began.
Think of the shrieking eagle on our van,
the decal, with its wings aflame,
and our prophetic name,
The Downward Spiral,
the viral
expansion of it,
the perks and packed arenas
before the groupies got between us,
the label dropped us, and the fad wound down.

Boys, since this bar is in a nowhere town,
let's pound out, with our amps cranked up to ten,
sincerer tribute to the angry art
than we could handle at our start.
The blasphemy we hurled
against the world
back then
was out of season.
Now we have damned good reason
to smash things up like ruined men,
and all my lyrics will be from the heart.

Stock and Bond

Since the recession my domestic
dream has been one bedroom, one bath,
a porch, a hammock and a path
cutting through weeds to the majestic
remnants of a Cadillac,
an ax stuck in a chopping block
and, further out, a rickety dock
where the companions I throw back
are always waiting to be fed—
gilded and silvered, carved from jade,
the whole fortune I never made,
shimmering in a pond, instead.

The Problem of Evil

A sharp-shinned hawk has clenched a perch
some yards shy of the weeping birch
from which your handmade birdhouse dangles.
The devil when it comes to angles,
he looks out for his interests.

Chickadees sporting flashy bibs
have blown in from abroad, their nibs
black blurs erasing the buffet.
Thanks in the key of *fee-bee-bay*
kicks up their caps and puffs their breasts.

You there sunning on the stoop
start at the shadow of a swoop.
The party scatters, minus one,
and Oh my God what have you done?
You built that house to serve its guests.

The Parlor

Nothing was an heirloom. We had none,
but a cause cherished like a vintage gun
hung there: why goatherds in a mountain town
had filed into a ditch and lain face-down.

I'm vicious even as a great grandson
when people tell me what was done is done.
Our women—raped not just by anyone.
We never called the couch an ottoman.

Kudzu: An Immigrant's Tale

Dirty Japanese
at customs, he reached out, copped
   feels of rocks and trees,

fences, an outhouse.
Then, once his neediness found
   a lace-curtain spouse

to carry his name,
he blent in, naturalized,
   and at length became

an up-and-comer
on hills, in hollers, greater
   summer by summer,

till all Dixieland
felt small. Where had he picked up
   this itch to expand?

From shoguns back home?
Noodling through our heady
   American loam?

A yen to wester
set off his tendrils and now,
   a vast investor,

   he has snatched up land
in Texas, Utah even.
   He's way out of hand,

   so far overgrown,
we must complain about him
   as one of our own.

Mrs. Pulaski's Shrine

Despite the drainpipe daily
bringing up bolder roaches,
and the imbalanced couches,
dragged in from the alley,
breeding mites and mice,
this shack is sacred space:

a doily marks the holy
of holies, and a vase
magnifies the lace,
and lilies-of-the-valley
from out of this world perfume
the one room, the whole home,

the whole soul of the place.

Off the Clock

Co-conspirators for an afternoon,
we gathered, hush-hush, at the slow café.
Last week was debts and earthquakes but today
nothing is pressing. If a coffee spoon
is stirring, if the shadows lengthen there
beyond the awning, or the daily news,
catching the breeze, rustles around our shoes,
our minds are absent, and we just don't care.

Blank for a space, we are the interval
that traffic whispers by. Still, though our lull
grows on a roadside, we will be vacations,

our lungs alone working in lieu of us,
breathing routinely as an empty bus
goes through the motions, brakes at vacant stations.

The Mentor

i.m. Alan Sullivan

You were a man intolerant of nonsense.
Your voice dug in, expanded and became my conscience.
  Now you shock me from beyond the grave.
I should be grateful someone's still around to save
  my moron forays from the Mire of Lies.
Truth is, every time a real hard-ass dies,
  the brunt of him just doesn't go away.
Truth is, you live on, killing all I shouldn't say.

The Vigil

Because he was as hard to handle
as truth, which we equate with light,
go somewhere dark and hold a candle
for Alan Sullivan tonight.

Captain Meriwether Lewis and the Great Falls

I was the one, the first white man, to shiver
into the wind of it—a rush so grand
it felt like God was barreling downriver.

I was the fool who marked in a clear hand
its height and spate, certain that words would claim
what savages had only scratched in sand.

I was an ass to fix it with a name.
What was the use? The blasted thing went on
thundering Shush! to spite me all the same.

After the portage, I sat up till dawn
ignoring what was missing, since I knew
that part of me had quit the corps and gone

to serve there, hushed and worshipping the view,
no matter what we went on to subdue.

Captain Meriwether Lewis at the Pacific

We toed the ocean, so the time had come.
Seagulls were seagulls. It was afternoon.
We had to head back where we started from.

Great men would praise me from the podium
just as they cheered, years back, a Daniel Boone
so broken to the ways of heathendom
that he ate dog and fumbled with a spoon.

There was the East but, when I would have swum
for Shanghai, fought even the wild monsoon,
duty deterred me from delirium.

Back home I hoped to drop whatever sum
my field notes fetched me on an air balloon
and sail off, with a basket full of rum,
for El Dorado, maybe, or the moon.

A Place in France

Matter

Darling, in France
some crank has whipped up
a black hole under
glass, and I worry:
what if he slipped up?
I mean, one blunder,
one mischance,
and the world will be sorry.

Will one vast gullet
suck the clock tower
sideways and pull it
out of time?
Will police headquarters
lose all power
at the end of crime?
Will ecstatic reporters
somehow contrive
to capture on tape
the rapid advance
of the Rapture, live?
Will nothing escape,
not even light?
Somewhere in France
it is not even night.

Sooner or later,
for better or worse,
a Re-Creator
will stop and reverse
motion, revamp
lab and lamp,
earth, sun and moon—
possibly soon.

Alive tonight
in Utah, dear,
with candlelight
and an atmosphere,
I hope my affection
will never shatter
or shift direction.
May such things matter.

Torque

This engine started in a courtyard where
three Russian girls in summer dresses took profound
drags and exhaled voluptuous gossip—air
rippled around them; benches were abuzz;
even a deaf man would have trembled at the sound.
I knew no Russian, so the message was:

syllables rough and smooth enough to soothe and stir,
we are the deep massage, the cosmic purr.

My brain turned over. Everything was turbulence.
This engine has been revving ever since.

Almond-Eyed

Sorry, I keep imagining you are,
way back along the spice road, a bazaar
exhaling myrrh, nutmeg and cinnamon
caravanned from the rising sun,
and turbaned buyers for Tuscan ateliers
  hauled saffron and vermilion
  out of your puffed pavilion
to give the Renaissance its dawns and days.

Charming, but of course why should you care
what I concoct out of your sensual air?
History to you was books but worse and more.
Vahr is the way you speak of war
because smashed windows, mobs and mortars drove you
  to Tver where Slavic pride
  spits on the almond-eyed.
And now some jerk is sniveling *I love you.*

Listen, the truth is love's a luxury.
I do not need you; you do not need me.
One could cook supper without salt or sauce
and soldier on despite the loss.
But what I mean is us, like sovereign states
  positioned side by side,
  thriving when unified,
eying their movements from our Lion Gates.

Chumps

Instead of saying you are
in some immediate danger,
some night club or sports car,
an anonymous stranger
armed with a soothing voice is
offering those who adore you
non-negotiable choices:

to leave a message for you,
we should please press one
or simply wait for the tone;
press star when we are done
or just hang up the phone.

To My Soul Mate

I like you fine. How could I not?
We toss the same frisbee of thought
then split a smoke. I find in you
my own dizzy imagination
and raillery's twin sister, sass,
and so, um, sex would feel taboo,
you know, like with a near relation.
I never kiss the looking glass.

Some seek themselves in others (thus
Hapsburgs and Appalachian hicks
considered siblings a good catch)
but we should breed exogamous
ingredients into our mix.
Fruitlessly, then, we make a match
like two left stockings or a word
trying to rhyme the same damn word.

You Klutz

Her gasp reversed and horror halting:

the cause, a spatter of Shiraz,
gathering back to impact on
her vintage cashmere sweater, vaulting
outthrown hand and rising rim,
swirling above the straightening stem,
dregs first, breath last—a giddy glass.

She's smiling, fresh from the salon.

Pulling the Wagon

Who left me here to babysit her?
There she goes crying—should I coddle
and soothe her? Run out of the room?
No one could kiss this boo-boo better.
Why shush her with another bottle,
swaddle her in my arms and hum?

Booze tastes best when the loss is bitter
and all love is a lasting battle.
Her parents crashed and won't come home.

The Last Bachelors

Over our booth at Club Quixote hung
a light bulb. Far side of the churning smoke
swam tragic Pat (our ironist and joke)
with handsome Raffi of the Honey Tongue.
Others had married but we held out yet,
the last bachelors and without regret,

so long as gaga gals with clacking bangles
passed in command of numerals and a name.
Though we, like pool sharks, spent most of the game
waiting our turn and wrangling over angles
we came up with some charming things to say
and hardly aged—until I drove away

to the insipid city Desolate
where girls are far too young or very married.
But I bet on the loss, boys, and I buried
my sweet talk back along the interstate
where Casanova and Squeaks the Randy Clown
haunt dusty barrooms in a dry ghost town.

Well, Since You Asked . . .

A homesick exile under an alpine range
I feel close to a summit—distant, blue.

Did you mean monkhood when you praised the change?
Not even God will talk to you-know-who.

Oh, and the locals? Blond, but too damn good,
too quick to tie the knot and weed the lawn.

Say Hello to the gang back in the 'hood
and pretty please think of me, or I'm gone.

Utah Adieu

Felicia's flight to Boston will be great
even if bumpy air upsets her stomach,
children are shrill, and flustered mothers mean,
even if she must sit sandwiched between
fat sweaty people on a backed-up tarmac,
panting for freedom and an open gate . . .

that is, her flight to Boston will be great
so long as she just goes. I cannot suffer
the outback when she's in it, cannot take
mountains of dryness and the Great Salt Lake.
Board, girl, embrace your more attractive offer.
Go force perfection on some other state.

The Plumbing

As a none-too-subtle rain
runs off and heaves itself
up through the shower drain,
and a swamp forms, a lake
lapping the moldings, a tide
high on the shoals of shoes
and continental shelf,
I lie far from awake,
dreaming of oceanside
embraces in Cancun.

Now I have blown a fuse.
The clock drowned, and it's noon
before the hedonist
with the see-through bathing suit on
vanishes in the mist.
What is that slosh? That draft?
Why is my darling futon
sea-level like a raft?

Water and sex and dreams
ran wild through the night
to send me a message, it seems:

Things are just not alright.
Vacate the basement, move
higher and start all over
with, at the least, a lover
and big enough bed for love.

To the Bride, in the Dressing Room

Since a crushed frill
would spoil your gown
and a tipsy spill
bring the day down,

stand where you are—
do not recline.
You have made it this far,
so cork the wine.

To alter as planned
and escape from stains
you must withstand,
for the stretch that remains,

heels (the infernal
humblers of height)
and time's eternal
war against white.

The march has begun.
Old pipes proclaim
your *per-fec-tion.*
Go yield your name

to the saint who could wait
for the bells to ring—
No, it's too late.
No, it's nothing.

You will find me outside,
eyes wet with the grit
that kept the bride
immaculate.

SAPPHO

Two Fragments

I.
Carpenters, raise the rafter-beam
(for Hymen's wedding hymn)
a little higher to make room
(for Hymen's wedding hymn)
because here comes the groom—
an Ares more imposing than
a giant, a terribly big man.

II.
and may the maidens all night long
celebrate your shared love in song
and the bride's bosom,
a violet blossom.

Get up, now! Rouse that gang of fellows—
your boys—and we shall sleep as well as
the bird that intones
piercing moans.

One Plus One: A Wedding Sermon

We find atop the summit of a march
the reason we have gathered here today
at odds: soft ruffle versus worsted starch;
his sharpness, her florescence. How can they,
each keeper of an obstinate ideal,
   merge to a round cube, a squared circle?
   We sit here waiting on a miracle.
These so-called weddings, how can they be real?

Disregard, first, that one plus one is two
and then, since lives are not like oil paints
readily swirling into something new,
assume an agent that breaks down constraints,
amps up attraction and proceeds to fuse.
   Sounds wild, I know, but you can see
   proof in the waves of energy
irradiating altar, aisle and pews.

So go on, bathe in them and offer presents
to what is giddy or gasping and what cries.
Breathe the bouquets that emanate their essence.
Hum when guitar and tenor harmonize.
Today the single cynic feels persuasion
   urging one plus one is one.
   Yes, something crazy has begun
among those mystics there, on this occasion.

The Long Window

Yes, dear, they're precious. We were like them once,
Amnion's unwilling emigrants
embraced by giants and the cold outside.
  Coo what you will, they clearly feel
  that breathing air's a rotten deal.
It's tough luck being washed up with the tide.

Granted, they shush when suckled from the loss
and settle down to juice and applesauce.
Colors distract them, dancing stimuli—
  numbers and letters, guns or dolls,
  the faces of the animals.
Some will be happy; most will multiply,

and that's the issue. We should spell it out:
you are the certitude, and I the doubt
wasting your time. We walk on a divide
  that runs midway from either shore.
  I don't get what we came here for.
Set a term—say, nine months to decide.

Places, Places

Two minutes, people . . . wait, hold, hold for ten.
Boots clomp and flounces rustle in distress:
the leading man has passed out drunk again.
And who are you? You'll have to do, I guess.

No use resisting—practiced hands have stripped me
and crammed my toes, hams, haunches into hose.
What lines, what cues, what songs? They have equipped me
only with rapier and mustachios.

Showtime. A hush blows in and lights discover
the cardboard forest where I must fool all
the people, all, at least till curtain call.

And then one step as hero, fop or lover,
and I have stumbled from the dream. It's dawn.
The setting is my own. The show goes on.

The Stage Designer

Director of the hands that would create
a quaint Spain for our tragic little affair,
she uttered, as her gestures carved from air,
stucco and tile for a grandee's estate,
coiffures, costumes, flesh for my libretto:
the too enticing wife in silk brocade
sang from the balcony; the rakish blade
held a bouquet, the cuckold a stiletto.

She spoke so well I had my own designs
until a sudden husband came to get her,
and that was it. *Good night.* (I cut some lines.)

And off they drove back to their own routines
and I to mine, and life may well be better
without the drama, the big ugly scenes.

The Bad Tree

Why was the bad tree so appealing?
Why did the fruit perspire so much?
Its musk reached out, a red-light touch
tugging them toward a funny feeling.

Their friend the snake spoke like his glide.
Who could refute such breathiness?
God never talked to them like this.
They gobbled, giggled, ran to hide.

All Eden gasped at the taboo:
what were those fig-leaves doing there?
Naughty and awkward, self-aware,
they kissed the beasts and left the zoo.

Soon as the wind got what they wore,
the bees were mean, and the birds, shy.
Exile was one big public eye.
So they devised, for shame, a door

that shut and house to shut it in,
ripped out a mess of moral thickets
and ringed with roses, rules and pickets
modesty in the midst of sin . . .

where you will find them to this day,
torn as their children err and learn
how tart rebellion tastes in turn.
We grow up fast and move away.

Spare Change

You know that heap out on the stoop? The grand
dame hollowed out by meth and destitution?
Well, when I paid the toll, she squeezed my hand
and fed me nonsense I could understand:

Love in the air's a kite cut from a string,
a red balloon, a sweet sort of pollution,
changing the world—that's how it seemed in spring.
It smells like aftershave or some such thing.

The Light at Troy

Medusa

I was out on the stoop that day
watching the swallows, braiding
my hair, not really waiting
for marriage or love or trouble,
when I was swept away
to the sanctum of a temple
and ruined. Horrid enough,
but then he just took off
and left me there to pay
everything for the crime
of sex in sacred space.

Flush with conviction, the marble
goddess stepped from her base
and wrecked me a second time
and handed me a mirror:
an orgy of snakes for hair,
a neolithic glare,
the horror, O the horror—
justice isn't fair.

What could I do, though? Mother,
sisters—everyone
I turned to turned to stone.
Monster like any other,
I shambled off alone.

No kisses, no goodbyes,
though on the last frontier
I spat three times and hurled
a curse at the garrison
that stands for civil order
and the whole known world.

Life is a dream out here
on the wild side of the border:
the sun is loath to rise,
and prides of sphinxes roam
freely among the crags,
and three prophetic hags
sit chuckling round a cauldron.
I dug a humble home
and learned to love my children,
my little wisps, the asps.

And years glide by, and ages,
under the light of torches
and we are content to tend
our gallery of the gorgeous
torsos who came to call,
arms with a fist or a weapon
and heads ranged on the wall
gaping with eyes wide open
at justice in the end.

The Marriage of Peleus and Thetis

Death is an evil—so the gods have judged.
Had it been good, they too would die.

Sappho

Petty as we are but more beautiful,
the goddesses could only squabble
over a gaudy bauble
and call us dull.

But we the drab mothers, the wedding-planners,
stood aloof and shrugged at their bad manners.
The world turned upside down: though bound for Hades,
we snubbed Heaven's Empress and the fancy ladies.
Gods were like mortals, mortals like the gods—
we paid them back in condescending nods.

They won all, though, and all we lost
by dying rankles
our ghostly bosoms: tossed
tresses, clacking bangles, dancing ankles.

Sappho

Some call ships, infantry or horsemen

Some call ships, infantry or horsemen
the greatest beauty earth can offer;
I say it is whatever a person
most lusts after.

Proving the point will be no trouble:
Helen surpassed all humankind
in looks but left the world's most noble
husband behind,

coasting off to Troy where she
thought nothing of her loving parents
and only child, but led astray . . .

. . . and I think of Anaktoria
far away . . .

and I would rather watch her body
sway, her glistening face flash dalliance
than Lydian war cars at the ready
and armed battalions.

Helen's *Iliad*

Yes, there were towers at Troy, and in one spire
they made me mistress of a little room
with windows. While the rind of their desire
played daughter-in-law and never left the loom,
I waged war in the warp threads, ranged afield
and rode on air:

                  a malformed metalworker
animates dancers on a flawless shield;
a mother arms her beautiful berserker;
gods tiff; and, as a river jumps its channel,
the blond boy slaughters myriads of men . . .

but final scenes are hard, and that last panel—
should I have wrought a world at peace again
where longtime rivals share a hearty laugh
or mowed my foes down, Greeks or Trojans bending
before the scythe, their bluster so much chaff?

My flight expired—torched towers the true ending,
and I suppose I loved both sides, depending.

Antiphon

That evening Antiphon the tavern warbler
debuted a ditty called *Horribler, Horribler:*

"Forward is backward; culture proved a waste.
Our patriarchs waged war at eighty, now
their sons send slaves. Back when our lusts were chaste
Nature was maidenly, but plow and prow
ravished the furrows of her lands and seas
for funny fruits that nourished more bad seed.
Taste made rakes, and today's necessities
are last week's luxuries and last month's greed.
Signs have arrived—the comet, the dire bird—
forecasting Thracians, maybe, or our first
raids from the East. Be wise, my comrades, gird
your loins, dig trenches and expect the worst.
It's late now, and there's nothing we can do."

The grumps nodded as if each word were true.

Meanwhile events ran along switch-back paths,
zigzagging up and down at no fixed rate:
where new ductwork facilitated baths
a son drowned a father for his estate
while, on the coast where Medes besieged defenses
to kill all who contested them by water,
a mother, reckoning the year's expenses,

resolved not to expose her newborn daughter—
such things were good or bad and would go on.

And as the crowd went on by fits and starts
catcalling and extolling Antiphon
a goatherd and a flute-girl (two sweethearts
who never would be rich or mean much harm)
yawned in the face of stylized despair
and, slipping off behind his master's farm,
lay in a hayloft and were happy there.

The Birth of Philosophy

Only the bustling harbor could afford
spare hours for unprofitable abstraction
in which elusive sea nymphs, traced backward
to ignoble births in sailors' fantasies,
absently lectured on Homeric fiction.

Slow, as the slight but actual advance
of stars in darkness, high tide on the cliff
ruled out the tinkering of deities,
the first philosopher: "What if . . . what if
we offer incense to indifference?"

The Mystes

Remember when they charged in beating spears on shields?
   And all us clods abandoning the fields
for what we thought was safety in the city walls?
   Too big a herd corralled in too few stalls
breeds pestilence, of course. And so, of course, a curse
   erupted, stiffs were everywhere and, worse,
the stink and vultures.
                                    Once back then I saw you go
   under the shadow of a portico
where this bald, sweaty scholar in a beggar's cloak
   kept stressing like the punch line of a joke:
nothingness, being nothing, is no thing to dread.
   Remember him? The way you shook your head
rocked my indifference, so I tried to cheer you up
   by singing *Life is brief, so pass the cup*
and *Human generations flourish and fall like leaves.*

   Then on the day they torched our barley sheaves
we torched our dead. Their smoke below, our smoke above it
   tarnished the air, and you were dying of it
because your wife was ashes who had done the baking.
   I caught you crushing hemlock first, then snaking
a rope around a rafter. All that zeal, my friend,
   so many means at hand, and in the end
you only signed up for those kooky mystery rites.

53

Absorbing you, the corps of neophytes
proceeded under treaty along the Sacred Way.
  I kept my distance but enjoyed the play
staged at the bridge: lewd leanings in steatopygian
  padding and strapped-on pricks. (At least religion
had sense enough to keep the entertainment light
  before a full day's fast and solemn night.)

Just shy of hallowed ground, on a cracked column drum,
  I sat watching you wait for dusk to come
all day. When Hesper showed at last, and the first bat,
  a sacred ladle skimmed a storage vat—
what was the draught the goddess offered? What weird brew
  woke your exhausted body or warped its view?

Torches ignited, pitch-pine resin tinged the air.
  Priestesses led you up and down, nowhere,
until the brands found sconces and the incense curled
  around the pillars of an Underworld
quarried from granite—Pluto's grotto, a grim room:
  When, at the urging of a tall dark groom,
a bride laid the bouquet aside and raised her veil
  her mother, above them, loosed a piercing wail.

Thus readied for the temple, the Telesterion,
  you climbed steps at a dead march and were gone.
Whatever happened—whether ears of grain were ground
  under a pestle, asps were passed around
or potent pomegranates opened and their arils

shared among all—you came out singing carols
at dawn, beaming beneath the victory wreath you wore.

The more power to you, buddy. Here's the score:
I'm scared. What was at first a little tickling cough
    has stuck deep, and I can't just shrug it off.
The dog has died, the donkey, now my brother-in-law.
    The deal's like this: you tell me what you saw,
and I'll forget about those shears you borrowed. No?
    How about thirty sheep? I'll even throw
some goats in—trifles if a man can sleep at ease.
    My wife? My cattle? Dammit, please, then . . . please?

SAPPHO

Girls, chase the violet-bosomed Muses' bright

Girls, chase the violet-bosomed Muses' bright
gifts and the plangent lyre, lover of hymns.

Stiffness has seized on these once supple limbs,
and black braids with the passing years turned white.

Age weighs heavily on me, and the knees
buckle that long ago, like fawns, pranced nimbly.

I groan much but to what end? Humans simply
cannot be ageless like divinities.

They say that rosy-forearmed Dawn, when stung
with love, swept a sweet youth to the earth's rim—

Tithonus. Even there age withered him,
bound still to a wife forever young.

Leonardo's *Madonna of the Rocks* (1485)

We missed the cataclysm, the old calm
rent at the advent of the love parade.
Fed on their presence, columbine and palm
sprouted from stone; stone sprouted a cascade.

Kneeling (but only for a picnic), Mary,
John and an angel pamper and distract
the rebel innocence no sanctuary,
no mother, friend or guardian can protect

as doom detonates *Annus Domini.*
Coarse codes are crumbling. In the *sfumato*
rock like the ruptured maw of some colossal
crocodile, some quaint, Draconian fossil.
Bethlehem felt the pang, and now this grotto
just off the Roman road to Calvary.

Metamorphic

Slabs of it traveled down a switchback path
to Roman Athens, waited in the square
until Andronikos the polymath
arrived with plans and built a tower there,

eight-sided, so the eight gods of the wind
could puff and pucker in distinctive scenes.
Although mere art once half the world had sinned,
they kept on puffing for the Byzantines,

who thought an octagon the ideal place
for baptisms—chrism and candle wax
anointing porous floors as peals of grace
rattled the ashlars, shook dust from the cracks.

After the crumbling of Christendom
the sheik stopped by at noon, and dervishes
put down their bowls, picked up a chime or drum
and chanted *God, God, God is all there is.*

Drawn, then, to the source of all perfections,
one in the center of concentric rings
whirled and whirled, a gust in all directions
filling the tower that had been many things.

In His Beak an Olive Branch

Come, chosen ones, admire the pigeon:
urban and secular, he perches
   on houses of religion,
mosques and synagogues and churches.

When mounted upon Mark the Lion
he coos no Latin to the lambs
   and thinks nothing of Zion
when settling its hexagrams.

Pillared in aniconic space,
he rules his roost and cannot care
   which way the faithful face
or what name hastens them to prayer.

Mecca, Jerusalem and Rome—
so much gibberish to a brain
   deprived of words for "home,"
"hereafter," "sacred" and "profane."

Whichever God we wield as judge,
the pigeon never takes offense
   and so can't bear a grudge.
Come, friends, envy his innocence.

Death and the Matron

A dusty dancing-floor, a paneled screen
   painted like a façade, and noon
denying depth to the climactic scene:
Death enters like a champion. Ahs and ohs
flutter like roses as he strikes a pose,
his sword poised for the blow. We know the queen
   has woken from her latest swoon
   because she must be dying soon
and needs to speak her piece before she goes.

God bless the lady—she will go down talking
   as if each passage were her last,
a swan singing a filibuster, blocking
the *coup de grâce*. One moment in suspense
spiraling outward into eloquence,
the plot curls up and dozes; Death stops stalking
   and stands with the supporting cast.
   It's too late now, she's bound us fast
with long sentences, coiled magnificence.

photo by Sumner Hatch

Aaron Poochigian was born in 1973. He attended Moorhead State University from 1991 to 1996 where he studied under the poets Tim Murphy, Dave Mason and Alan Sullivan. He entered graduate school for Classics in 1997 at the University of Minnesota. After traveling and doing research in Greece on fellowship from 2003 to 2004, he earned a Ph.D. in Classics in 2006, and now lives and writes in New York City.

His translations, with introduction and notes, of Sappho's poems and fragments were published by Penguin Classics in 2009. His translations of Aeschylus, Aratus and Apollonius of Rhodes appeared in the *Norton Anthology of Greek Literature in Translation* in the spring of 2009, and Johns Hopkins University Press published his edition of Aratus' astronomical poem, *The Phaenomena,* with his introduction and notes, in the spring of 2010. His poetry has appeared in numerous journals, including *Arion, The Dark Horse, Poetry* and *Smartish Pace.*

www.ingramcontent.com/pod-product-compliance
Lightning Source LLC
Chambersburg PA
CBHW022149090426
42742CB00010B/1441